Ducks, Bucks, and Woodchucks

by Dave Miller, Ph.D.

A.P. "Learn to Read" Series

God made ducks.

Ducks swim.

Ducks like to swim in lakes and ponds.

Ducks do not cluck.

Ducks quack.

Ducks are soft.

God made ducks.

God made bucks.

A buck is a deer.

A buck is a boy deer.

A doe is a girl deer.

A buck can grow horns.

Horns are antlers (ANT-lers).

God made bucks.

God made woodchucks.

Woodchucks like to dig.

They have long claws.

Woodchucks like to climb.

Woodchucks like to climb trees.

Woodchucks live in a den.

God made
woodchucks.

God made ducks, bucks and woodchucks.

God made them all.

God made them all on days five and six.

God is good!

The "Learn to Read" Series: A Word to Parents

Rationale: To provide books for children (ages 3-6) from Christian homes for the purpose of assisting them in **learning to read** while simultaneously introducing them to the **Creator** and His **creation.**

Difficulty Level

The following listing provides a breakdown of the number and length of words in *Ducks, Bucks, and Woodchucks* (not counting plurals and duplicates):

Total Number of Words: 44

1—One letter word
a

5—Two letters words
to, in, do, is, on

12—Three letter words
God, and, not, are, boy, doe,
can, dig, den, all, day, six

21—Four letter words
made, duck, swim, like, lake, pond, soft, buck,
deer, girl, grow, horn, they, have, long, claw,
tree, live, them, five, good

3—Five letter words
cluck, quack, climb

1—Six letter word
antler

1—Eight letter word
woodchuck

**Drawings by
Cana Hallenbeck, Age 8**

The A.P. Readers

LEVEL 1 — "Learn to Read"

1. Dogs, Frogs, and Hogs
2. Bats, Cats, and Rats
3. Birds, Bugs, and Bees
4. Fish, Flies, and Fleas
5. Goose, Moose, and Mongoose
6. Ducks, Bucks, and Woodchucks
7. Snails, Quails, and Whales

LEVEL 2 — "Early Reader"

1. God Made the World
2. God Made Reptiles
3. God Made Animals
4. God Made Insects
5. God Made Plants
6. God Made Fish
7. God Made You

LEVEL 3 — "Advanced Reader"

1. Amazing Tamable Animals
2. Amazing Tails
3. Amazing Dinosaurs
4. The Amazing Human Body
5. Amazing Migrating Animals
6. Amazing Copies of God's Design
7. Amazing Teeth

We continue to expand the number of titles in each series. Be sure to check our Web site for our newest books.

www.ApologeticsPress.org